Dear John

I don't know if [you have]
read Kalil Gibran but I am taking the
chance. (or it can just become an impressive
dust collector on your book shelf.) I glanced
through the book, reading some of the brief
stories. I hope that they give you strength &
add to your understanding of Life rather
than be life-denying for you.

Thank you for including me in the
Easter Eve / Baptism service at St. Mary's.
It was quite wonderful & a new experience
for me. (you noticed – I stayed until the end)
– the music, the ritual of dark & light & so
much more. I wasn't sure why nor how
the scriptures from the Old Testament
were chosen.

I hope that the evening was moving for
you & that you felt the presence & legacy
of your dad with you.

This is the beginning of another
chapter of your life journey & deepening
faith.

Blessings..
Mary Lou (Shortell)

TEARS
and
LAUGHTER

Kahlil Gibran

TEARS
and
LAUGHTER

CASTLE BOOKS

To M.E.H.

I present this book—first breeze in the tempest
of my life—to that noble spirit who walks
with the tempest and loves with the breeze.

KAHLIL GIBRAN

This edition copyright © 1993 by Castle Books,
a division of Book Sales, Inc.
114 Northfield Avenue
Edison, NJ 08837

Reprinted by permission and agreement of
Carol Publishing Group
600 Madison Avenue
New York, NY 10022

Printed in the United States of America

ISBN 0-7858-1072-2

Contents

EDITOR'S PREFACE   7

FOREWORD   13

THE CREATION   15

HAVE MERCY ON ME, MY SOUL!   17

TWO INFANTS   20

THE LIFE OF LOVE   22

THE HOUSE OF FORTUNE   25

SONG OF THE WAVE   26

A POET'S DEATH IS HIS LIFE   28

PEACE   30

THE CRIMINAL   32

THE PLAYGROUND OF LIFE   34

SONG OF FORTUNE   36

THE CITY OF THE DEAD   38

SONG OF THE RAIN   40

THE WIDOW AND HER SON   42

THE POET   44

SONG OF THE SOUL   46

LAUGHTER AND TEARS   48

SONG OF THE FLOWER   51

VISION   53

THE VICTORS   55

SONG OF LOVE   59

TWO WISHES   61

SONG OF MAN   63

YESTERDAY AND TODAY   65

BEFORE THE THRONE OF BEAUTY   68

LEAVE ME, MY BLAMER   70

A Lover's Call   73

The Beauty of Death   76

The Palace and the Hut   80

A Poet's Voice   81

The Bride's Bed   87

Editor's Preface

KAHLIL GIBRAN might well have been an ancient, for the delicacy of his mind, the observations of his inner eyes, and the broad wisdom of his every parable. To ponder his profound approach to the complexities of life and then realize his recency to this world presents a momentary incongruity. It is soon lost, however, for Gibran is of all ages.

The advanced thought expressed in his rich, perceptive manner of thinking aloud slowly is characteristic of the mystics of the East, who devoted themselves to intensity of thought development. His mental meandering pursues a course that enables him to set forth the most intricate and deep-set ideas and problems in the simplest of language and understanding, and this quality, sought by so many and possessed by so few, paradoxically places Gibran many years into the future.

It is actually astounding that this, "the first breeze in the tempest of his life," with its obvious historical influence, tremendous philosophical significance, metaphysical probings, and ripe appreciation of life was written when he was scarcely twenty years old. He forces a sharp insistence to recall Plato and Goethe, whose classic works emerged in youth. As has been observed through later of his books, already published and widely read, this early brilliance was largely sustained throughout his tear-enriched life.

Principal among the additions to this new and enlarged edition is the strangely gripping story, *The Bride's Bed,* actually an eye-witness account of the incident related. Its theme is not new to the multitude of readers and students of Gibran, for the vicious inequality of man and woman had long been the object of his angriest literary attacks. One of the world's most fervent and outspoken champions of the cause of human

7

rights, Gibran had waged a long and bitter struggle to strengthen the recognition of youth's freedom of action in love, and to abolish from the social structure of the Middle East some of the ancient marriage customs prevailing. Particularly strong was his condemnation of the tradition of pre-arranged marriages of children by their parents, in complete disregard of the wishes and reactions of those so betrothed. It is a matter of common knowledge that these "transactions" often took place when the children concerned were scarcely old enough to walk, much less realize the enormous significance of the steps then being planned irrevocably for them. The ill-fated Lyla in this story, with courageous, anguished heroism, broke in unrestrained fury from this custom, bringing upon herself—fully anticipated—consequences so tragic, so far-reaching as to establish beyond question the widespread, deep-rooted nature of this practice in all of its personal, social, political, and ironically enough, even religious ramifications. Examine, for instance, the words of the priest addressed to the throng gathered about the lifeless bodies of the bride and the man she had really loved:

Cursed are the hands that touch these blood-spattered carcasses that are soaked with sin. And cursed are the eyes that shed tears of sorrow upon these two evil souls. Let the corpse of the son of Sodom and that of the daughter of Gomorrah remain lying in this diseased spot until the beasts devour their flesh and the wind scatters their bones. Go back to your homes and flee from the pollution of these sinners! Disperse now, before the flames of hell sting you, and he who remains here shall be cursed and excommunicated from the church and shall never again enter the temple and join the Christians in offering prayers to God!

It is a story of truth, of bravery, of all humanity's interest, going to the very core of individual liberty, and it is recognized conclusively by authorities the world over that Gibran, through the knife-edged at-

8

tacks of this story and others, was largely responsible for many of the social, political and religious reforms finally undertaken by the rulers of the East.

*   *   *   *

While it may appear, then, that we have in Kahlil Gibran a man who vacillates from the delicate to the strong, from the delightful to the frightening, from the lacy sweetness to the bitter condemnation, this chilling, magnetic mental roving is essentially the heart of his greatness, for his Psalm-like, exquisite poetry, catapulting swiftly to the unleashed vituperation of a Dante or Voltaire is the style that millions of readers in dozens of languages acknowledge as the most fascinating in all literary history. Any endeavor to categorize these writings, or to establish a source of influence, can result only in utter despair, for they are as strange and unorthodox as they are beautiful. As experts at the University of Oklahoma phrased it, *Gibran could write timeless truths in a way that makes the reader feel he is taking a walk in a quiet wood, or bathing in a cool stream; it soothes the spirit. But he could also write with a scorch like fire.*

These diametric opposites in the substance of his words presented no apparent difficulty to this master of simple, effective conveyance of thought, for, indicative of literary artistry, the flowing beauty of his lyrics does not palliate the strength of his indictments; nor does his execrating bitterness invade the gorgeous quality of his poetry, which has an appeal comparable to that of rich music.

His warnings are neither crusades nor preachments, yet every thought is conveyed completely, clearly, dynamically. He muses over the beautiful, not the ugly, and all of his criticisms are imbued with a gentle melancholy, subordinated finally to his magnificent descriptive powers, abounding with fine, metaphorical terseness.

Recent world developments have heightened interest in Arabic literature to a surprising degree, and English-

9

speaking peoples today are making deep, exploratory studies of these venerable writings, as yet unspoiled by Western influence.

The Arabs, despite centuries of internal political turbulence and external interference, have retained and improved their strong aesthetic and imaginative spirit. While the Western world has been looking at life and seeking practical solutions to its problems through religion and science, the various peoples comprising Arabia have preferred to indulge primarily in poetic and philosophical thinking. Under a cultural climate determined by the indigenous doctrines of Mohammed and those following him, the Arab writers have captured intact the spirit of their people, portraying the filial piety of the home, and the blind fidelity of all to their rulers, right or wrong. Never having suffered under religious bias nor adhered to scientific theories, Arabic writers have felt a freedom of expression of which the Western literati may well be envious. They set their own unconventional pattern, and no amount of outside pressure or criticism has been able to divert them from it. In the present pursuit of greater learning in Arabic writings, no author of the East offers greater reward than does Kahlil Gibran, for he stands alone on the summit of all that is fine in Sufi literature.

Reference has been made to Gibran's youth at the time of these writings, and this factor cannot be regarded lightly, for it renders all the more remarkable his ripe and mature grasp on a subject that has baffled and intrigued philosophers and thinkers from the beginning— the destiny of man, and the tremendous *why* of his being. Likewise, his unquestioned mastery of the art of symbolism and simile, sparkling in profusion throughout *Tears and Laughter,* is a tribute to his astounding stature in literary accomplishment, for this is an achievement that few, at any age, have been able to attain. His sympathetic approach to the prospect of death is also a creature of the mind belonging to the aged, but a knowledge of Gibran's love for tears, as set forth in his foreword to this book, as well as his deep, sincere affection

for fellow sufferers, offer philosophically pleasant con-
templations of death. Many instances of real knowledge
of maturity and stability in marriage, despite his years,
come forth in the stories and poems that comprise this
volume. In *The Life of Love*, a poem likening the four
seasons of the year to the comparable periods of married
life, the aging couple exchanges reminiscences in winter
time, the husband affectionately sighing:

> *Feed the lamp with oil and let it not dim, and*
> *Place it by you, so I can read with tears what*
> *Your life with me has written upon your face.*
> *Bring Autumn's wine. Let us drink and sing the*
> *Song of remembrance to Spring's carefree sowing,*
> *And Summer's watchful tending, and Autumn's*
> *Reward in harvest.*
> *Come close to me, oh beloved of my soul; the*
> *Fire is cooling and fleeing under the ashes.*
> *Embrace me, for I feel loneliness; the lamp is*
> *Dim, and the wine which we pressed is closing*
> *Our eyes. Let us look upon each other before*
> *They are shut.*

Surprisingly, the mysticism that characterizes much of
Gibran's writing is found not in his poetry, where it
would be granted a great latitude of expression through
the very nature of poetic freedom, but in his prose
stories exclusively. This feature of his works is not a de-
terrent to reader interest, for his depth establishes itself
at a level of complete lucidity to all who endeavor to
find it, and his frequent voyages into the field of mys-
ticism supplement with spiritual argument the precepts
of his earthly discourses. His blending of oriental and
occidental philosophy is occasionally disconcerting to the
Western mind. One invariably has the feeling that the
emotions expressed so plainly were too large for words,
and were wrenched from him reluctantly through his
soul's compulsion. One cannot fail to recognize in him
the strong expression of a passionate urge to improve the
lot of suffering, exploited humanity, an impulse that fired
his mind and heart from childhood. It is a message,

11

moreover, that emanates from painful, soul-searing knowledge of man's inhumanity to man, drawn from a poignant memory of what his eyes had seen and his ears had heard in his close observance of the perpetual human tragedy. He conveys his sense of sorrow for the cruel waste of youth and beauty and talent and sensitivity implicit in the neglect and degradation of the millions throughout the East.

But far more than local evils and the abuse of power by Eastern regimes is woven into the living fabric of Gibran's verbal tapestry. With the moving intensity that characterizes truly significant utterance, his earliest—like his latest—writings project timeless, universal truths. And these are often presented in the captivating literary form of the parable, peculiarly a heritage of the ancient Aramaic tradition.

His sentiments herein give new force to his other great works, for all possess the power and effectiveness of his one enormous theme. They stress the generally understood, yet completely ignored fact that but few things in life have real importance. Again and again this Lebanese Savant reminds us that if human relationships are wrong, no other factors of life can really matter. For what power, or wealth, or prestige can compensate for the silent agony of the heart's bereavement? In what fashion can existence on earth be fulfilled when love departs or friendship withers? The bonds of a common brotherhood without demarcation, no less than personal and family ties, must be strengthened if, individually and collectively, we are to meet competently the challenge of progress—or even of survival itself.

Gibran drives these teachings forcefully to the heart, and they persist in agitating the heart to complete accord. Like Beethoven's deathless music, of which the composer said, "From the heart it has sprung, and to the heart it shall penetrate," these writings, through their own rich sincerity, reach the deepest recesses of our emotional and spiritual awareness.

MARTIN L. WOLF

New York City

Foreword

I WOULD NOT exchange the laughter of my heart for the fortunes of the multitudes; nor would I be content with converting my tears, invited by my agonized self, into calm. It is my fervent hope that my whole life on this earth will ever be tears and laughter.

Tears that purify my heart and reveal to me the secret
   of life and its mystery,
Laughter that brings me closer to my fellow men;
Tears with which I join the broken-hearted,
Laughter that symbolizes joy over my very existence.

I prefer death through happiness a thousandfold to life in vain and in despair.

An eternal hunger for love and beauty is my desire; I know now that those who possess bounty alone are naught but miserable, but to my spirit the sighs of lovers are more soothing than music of the lyre.

When night comes, the flower folds its petals and slumbers with Love, and at dawn, it opens its lips to receive the Sun's kisses, bespeckled by quick dartings of clouds which come, but surely go.

The life of flowers is hope and fulfillment and peace; tears and laughter.

The water disappears and ascends until it turns into clouds that gather upon the hills and valleys; and when it meets the breeze, it falls down upon the fields and joins the brook that sings its way toward the sea.

The life of clouds is a life of farewell and a life of reunion; tears and laughter.

Thus the spirit separates itself from the body and walks into the world of substance, passing like clouds

over the valleys of sorrow and mountains of happiness
until it meets the breeze of death and returns to its
starting place, the endless ocean of love and beauty
which is God.

The Creation

THE GOD separated a spirit from Himself and fashioned it into beauty. He showered upon her all the blessings of gracefulness and kindness. He gave her the cup of happiness and said, "Drink not from this cup unless you forget the past and the future, for happiness is naught but the moment." And He also gave her a cup of sorrow and said, "Drink from this cup and you will understand the meaning of the fleeting instants of the joy of life for sorrow ever abounds."

And the God bestowed upon her a love that would desert her forever upon her first sigh of earthly satisfaction, and a sweetness that would banish with her first awareness of flattery.

And He gave her wisdom from heaven to lead her to the all-righteous path, and placed in the depth of her heart an eye that sees the unseen, and created in her an affection and goodness toward all things. He dressed her with raiment of hopes spun by the angels of heaven from the sinews of the rainbow. And He cloaked her in the shadow of confusion, which is the dawn of life and light.

Then the God took consuming fire from the furnace of anger, and searing wind from the desert of ignorance, and sharp-cutting sands from the shore of selfishness, and coarse earth from under the feet of ages, and combined them all and fashioned Man. He gave to Man a blind power that rages and drives him into a madness which extinguishes only before gratification of desire, and placed life in him which is the specter of death.

And the God laughed and cried. He felt an overwhelming love and pity for Man, and sheltered him beneath His guidance.

Have Mercy on Me, My Soul.

WHY ARE you weeping, my Soul?
Knowest thou my weakness?
Thy tears strike sharp and injure,
For I know not my wrong.
Until when shalt thou cry?
I have naught but human words
To interpret your dreams,
Your desires, and your instructions.

Look upon me, my Soul; I have
Consumed my full life heeding
Your teachings. Think of how
I suffer! I have exhausted my
Life following you.

My heart was glorying upon the
Throne, but is now yoked in slavery;
My patience was a companion, but
Now contends against me;
My youth was my hope, but
Now reprimands my neglect.

Why, my Soul, are you all-demanding?
I have denied myself pleasure
And deserted the joy of life
Following the course which you
Impelled me to pursue.
Be just to me, or call Death
To unshackle me,
For justice is your glory.

Have mercy on me, my Soul.
You have laden me with Love until
I cannot carry my burden. You and

Love are inseparable might; Substance
And I are inseparable weakness.
Will e'er the struggle cease
Between the strong and the weak?

Have mercy on me, my Soul.
You have shown me Fortune beyond
My grasp. You and Fortune abide on
The mountain top; Misery and I are
Abandoned together in the pit of
The valley. Will e'er the mountain
And the valley unite?

Have mercy on me, my Soul.
You have shown me Beauty, but then
Concealed her. You and Beauty live
In the light; Ignorance and I are
Bound together in the dark. Will
E'er the light invade darkness?

Your delight comes with the Ending,
And you revel now in anticipation;
But this body suffers with life
While in life.
This, my Soul, is perplexing.

You are hastening toward Eternity,
But this body goes slowly toward
Perishment. You do not wait for him,
And he cannot go quickly.
This, my Soul, is sadness.

You ascend high, through heaven's
Attraction, but this body falls by
Earth's gravity. You do not console
Him, and he does not appreciate you.
This, my Soul, is misery.

You are rich in wisdom, but this
Body is poor in understanding.

You do not compromise
And he does not obey.
This, my Soul, is extreme suffering.

In the silence of the night you visit
The Beloved and enjoy the sweetness of
His presence. This body ever remains
The bitter victim of hope and separation.
This, my Soul, is agonizing torture.
Have mercy on me, my Soul!

Two Infants

A PRINCE stood on the balcony of his palace addressing a great multitude summoned for the occasion and said, "Let me offer you and this whole fortunate country my congratulations upon the birth of a new prince who will carry the name of my noble family, and of whom you will be justly proud. He is the new bearer of a great and illustrious ancestry, and upon him depends the brilliant future of this realm. Sing and be merry!" The voices of the throngs, full of joy and thankfulness, flooded the sky with exhilarating song, welcoming the new tyrant who would affix the yoke of oppression to their necks by ruling the weak with bitter authority, and exploiting their bodies and killing their souls. For that destiny, the people were singing and drinking ecstatically to the health of the new Emir.

Another child entered life and that kingdom at the same time. While the crowds were glorifying the strong and belittling themselves by singing praise to a potential despot, and while the angels of heaven were weeping over the people's weakness and servitude, a sick woman was thinking. She lived in an old, deserted hovel and, lying in her hard bed beside her newly-born infant wrapped with ragged swaddles, was starving to death. She was a penurious and miserable young wife neglected by humanity; her husband had fallen into the trap of death set by the prince's oppression, leaving a solitary woman to whom God had sent, that night, a tiny companion to prevent her from working and sustaining life.

As the mass dispersed and silence was restored to the vicinity, the wretched woman placed the infant on her lap and looked into his face and wept as if she were to baptize him with tears. And with a hunger-weakened voice she spoke to the child saying, "Why have you left the spiritual world and come to share with me the bitterness of earthly life? Why have you deserted the angels and the spacious firmament and come to this miserable land of humans, filled with agony, oppression, and heartlessness? I have nothing to give you except tears; will you be nourished on tears instead of milk? I have no silk clothes to put on you; will my naked, shivering arms give you warmth? The little animals graze in the pasture and return safely to their shed; and the small birds pick the seeds and sleep placidly between the branches. But you, my beloved, have naught save a loving but destitute mother."

Then she took the infant to her withered breast and clasped her arms around him as if wanting to join the two bodies in one, as before. She lifted her burning eyes slowly toward heaven and cried, "God! Have mercy on my unfortunate countrymen!"

At that moment the clouds floated from the face of the moon, whose beams penetrated the transom of that poor home and fell upon two corpses.

Spring

COME, my beloved; let us walk amidst the knolls,
For the snow is water, and Life is alive from its
Slumber and is roaming the hills and valleys.
Let us follow the footprints of Spring into the
Distant fields, and mount the hilltops to draw
Inspiration high above the cool green plains.

Dawn of Spring has unfolded her winter-kept garment
And placed it on the peach and citrus trees; and
They appear as brides in the ceremonial custom of
The Night of Kedre.

The sprigs of grapevine embrace each other like
Sweethearts, and the brooks burst out in dance
Between the rocks, repeating the song of joy;
And the flowers bud suddenly from the heart of
Nature, like foam from the rich heart of the sea.

Come, my beloved; let us drink the last of Winter's
Tears from the cupped lilies, and soothe our spirits
With the shower of notes from the birds, and wander
In exhilaration through the intoxicating breeze.

Let us sit by that rock, where violets hide; let us
Pursue their exchange of the sweetness of kisses.

Summer

Let us go into the fields, my beloved, for the
Time of harvest approaches, and the sun's eyes
Are ripening the grain.
Let us tend the fruit of the earth, as the
Spirit nourishes the grains of Joy from the
Seeds of Love, sowed deep in our hearts.

Let us fill our bins with the products of
Nature, as life fills so abundantly the
Domain of our hearts with her endless bounty.
Let us make the flowers our bed, and the
Sky our blanket, and rest our heads together
Upon pillows of soft hay.
Let us relax after the day's toil, and listen
To the provoking murmur of the brook.

Autumn

Let us go and gather the grapes of the vineyard
For the winepress, and keep the wine in old
Vases, as the spirit keeps Knowledge of the
Ages in eternal vessels.

Let us return to our dwelling, for the wind has
Caused the yellow leaves to fall and shroud the
Withering flowers that whisper elegy to Summer.
Come home, my eternal sweetheart, for the birds
Have made pilgrimage to warmth and left the chilled
Prairies suffering pangs of solitude. The jasmine
And myrtle have no more tears.

Let us retreat, for the tired brook has
Ceased its song; and the bubblesome springs
Are drained of their copious weeping; and
The cautious old hills have stored away
Their colorful garments.
Come, my beloved; Nature is justly weary
And is bidding her enthusiasm farewell
With quiet and contented melody.

Winter

Come close to me, oh companion of my full life;
Come close to me and let not Winter's touch
Enter between us. Sit by me before the hearth,
For fire is the only fruit of Winter.

Speak to me of the glory of your heart, for
That is greater than the shrieking elements

Beyond our door.
Bind the door and seal the transoms, for the
Angry countenance of the heaven depresses my
Spirit, and the face of our snow-laden fields
Makes my soul cry.

Feed the lamp with oil and let it not dim, and
Place it by you, so I can read with tears what
Your life with me has written upon your face.
Bring Autumn's wine. Let us drink and sing the
Song of remembrance to Spring's carefree sowing,
And Summer's watchful tending, and Autumn's
Reward in harvest.

Come close to me, oh beloved of my soul; the
Fire is cooling and fleeing under the ashes.
Embrace me, for I fear loneliness; the lamp is
Dim, and the wine which we pressed is closing
Our eyes. Let us look upon each other before
They are shut.
Find me with your arms and embrace me; let
Slumber then embrace our souls as one.
Kiss me, my beloved, for Winter has stolen
All but our moving lips.

You are close by me, My Forever.
How deep and wide will be the ocean of Slumber;
And how recent was the dawn!

The House of Fortune

My wearied heart bade me farewell and left for the House of Fortune. As he reached that holy city which the soul had blessed and worshiped, he commenced wondering, for he could not find what he had always imagined would be there. The city was empty of power, money, and authority.

And my heart spoke to the daughter of Love saying, "Oh Love, where can I find Contentment? I heard that she had come here to join you."

And the daughter of Love responded, "Contentment has already gone to preach her gospel in the city, where greed and corruption are paramount; we are not in need of her."

Fortune craves not Contentment, for it is an earthly hope, and its desires are embraced by union with objects, while Contentment is naught but heartfelt.

The eternal soul is never contented; it ever seeks exaltation. Then my heart looked upon Life of Beauty and said, "Thou art all knowledge; enlighten me as to the mystery of Woman." And he answered, "Oh human heart, woman is your own reflection, and whatever you are, she is; wherever you live, she lives; she is like religion if not interpreted by the ignorant, and like a moon, if not veiled with clouds, and like a breeze, if not poisoned with impurities."

And my heart walked toward Knowledge, the daughter of Love and Beauty, and said, "Bestow upon me wisdom, that I might share it with the people." And she responded, "Say not wisdom, but rather fortune, for real fortune comes not from outside, but begins in the Holy of Holies of life. Share of thyself with the people."

Song of the Wave

THE STRONG SHORE is my beloved
And I am his sweetheart.
We are at last united by love, and
Then the moon draws me from him.
I go to him in haste and depart
Reluctantly, with many
Little farewells.

I steal swiftly from behind the
Blue horizon to cast the silver of
My foam upon the gold of his sand, and
We blend in melted brilliance.

I quench his thirst and submerge his
Heart; he softens my voice and subdues
My temper.
At dawn I recite the rules of love upon
His ears, and he embraces me longingly.

At eventide I sing to him the song of
Hope, and then print smooth kisses upon
His face; I am swift and fearful, but he
Is quiet, patient, and thoughtful. His
Broad bosom soothes my restlessness.

As the tide comes we caress each other,
When it withdraws, I drop to his feet in
Prayer.

Many times have I danced around mermaids
As they rose from the depths and rested
Upon my crest to watch the stars;
Many times have I heard lovers complain
Of their smallness, and I helped them to sigh.

Many times have I teased the great rocks
And fondled them with a smile, but never
Have I received laughter from them;
Many times have I lifted drowning souls
And carried them tenderly to my beloved
Shore. He gives them strength as he
Takes mine.

Many times have I stolen gems from the
Depths and presented them to my beloved
Shore. He takes in silence, but still
I give for he welcomes me ever.

In the heaviness of night, when all
Creatures seek the ghost of Slumber, I
Sit up, singing at one time and sighing
At another. I am awake always.

Alas! Sleeplessness has weakened me!
But I am a lover, and the truth of love
Is strong.
I may weary, but I shall never die.

A Poet's Death Is His Life

THE DARK WINGS of night enfolded the city upon which Nature had spread a pure and white garment of snow; and men deserted the streets for their houses in search of warmth, while the north wind probed in contemplation of laying waste the gardens. There in the suburb stood an old hut heavily laden with snow and on the verge of falling. In a dark recess of that hovel was a poor bed in which a dying youth was lying, staring at the dim light of his oil lamp, made to flicker by the entering winds. He was a man in the spring of life who foresaw fully that the peaceful hour of freeing himself from the clutches of life was fast nearing. He was awaiting Death's visit gratefully, and upon his pale face appeared the dawn of hope; and on his lips a sorrowful smile; and in his eyes forgiveness.

He was a poet perishing from hunger in the city of living rich. He was placed in the earthly world to enliven the heart of man with his beautiful and profound sayings. He was a noble soul, sent by the Goddess of Understanding to soothe and make gentle the human spirit. But alas! He gladly bade the cold earth farewell without receiving a smile from its strange occupants.

He was breathing his last and had no one at his bedside save the oil lamp, his only companion, and some parchments upon which he had inscribed his heart's feeling. As he salvaged the remnants of his withering strength he lifted his hands heavenward; he moved his eyes hopelessly, as if wanting to penetrate the ceiling in order to see the stars from behind the veil of clouds.

And he said, 'Come, oh beautiful Death; my soul is longing for you. Come close to me and unfasten the irons of life, for I am weary of dragging them. Come, oh sweet Death, and deliver me from my neighbors who looked upon me as a stranger because I interpret to them the language of the angels. Hurry, oh peaceful Death, and carry me from these multitudes who left me in the dark corner of oblivion because I do not bleed the weak as they do. Come, oh gentle Death, and enfold me under your white wings, for my fellowmen are not in want of me. Embrace me, oh Death, full of love and mercy; let your lips touch my lips which never tasted a mother's kiss, nor touched a sister's cheeks, nor caressed a sweetheart's fingertips. Come and take me, my beloved Death."

Then, at the bedside of the dying poet appeared an angel who possessed a supernatural and divine beauty, holding in her hand a wreath of lilies. She embraced him and closed his eyes so he could see no more, except with the eye of his spirit. She impressed a deep and long and gently withdrawn kiss that left an eternal smile of fulfillment upon his lips. Then the hovel became empty and nothing was left save parchments and papers which the poet had strewn about with bitter futility.

Hundreds of years later, when the people of the city arose from the diseased slumber of ignorance and saw the dawn of knowledge, they erected a monument in the most beautiful garden of the city and celebrated a feast every year in honor of that poet, whose writings had freed them. Oh, how cruel is man's ignorance!

Peace

THE TEMPEST calmed after bending the branches of the trees and leaning heavily upon the grain in the field. The stars appeared as broken remnants of the lightning, but now silence prevailed over all, as if Nature's war had never been fought.

At that hour a young woman entered her chamber and knelt by her bed sobbing bitterly. Her heart flamed with agony but she could finally open her lips and say, "Oh Lord, bring him home safely to me. I have exhausted my tears and can offer no more, oh Lord, full of love and mercy. My patience is drained and calamity is seeking possession of my heart. Save him, oh Lord, from the iron paws of War; deliver him from such unmerciful Death, for 'he is weak, governed by the strong. Oh Lord, save my beloved, who is thine own son, from the foe, who is thy foe. Keep him from the forced pathway to Death's door; let him see me, or come and take me to him."

Quietly a young man entered. His head was wrapped in bandage soaked with escaping life.

He approached her with a greeting of tears and laughter, then took her hand and placed against it his flaming lips. And with a voice which bespoke past sorrow, and joy of union, and uncertainty of her reaction, he said, "Fear me not, for I am the object of your plea. Be glad, for Peace has carried me back safely to you, and humanity has restored what greed essayed to take from us. Be not sad, but smile, my beloved. Do not express bewilderment, for Love has power that dispels Death; charm that conquers the enemy. I am your one. Think me not a specter emerging from the House of Death to visit your Home of Beauty.

Do not be frightened, for I am now Truth, spared from swords and fire to reveal to the people the triumph of

Love over War. I am Word uttering introduction to the play of happiness and peace."

Then the young man became speechless and his tears spoke the language of the heart; and the angels of Joy hovered about that dwelling, and the two hearts restored the singleness which had been taken from them.

At dawn the two stood in the middle of the field, contemplating the beauty of Nature injured by the tempest. After a deep and comforting silence, the soldier looked to the east and said to his sweetheart, "Look at the Darkness, giving birth to the Sun."

The Criminal

A YOUNG man of strong body, weakened by hunger, sat on the walker's portion of the street stretching his hand toward all who passed, begging and repeating the sad song of his defeat in life, while suffering from hunger and from humiliation.

When night came, his lips and tongue were parched, while his hand was still as empty as his stomach.

He gathered himself and went out from the city, where he sat under a tree and wept bitterly. Then he lifted his puzzled eyes to heaven while hunger was eating his inside, and he said, "Oh Lord, I went to the rich man and asked for employment, but he turned away because of my shabbiness; I knocked at the school door, but was forbidden solace because I was empty-handed; I sought any occupation that would give me bread, but all to no avail. In desperation I asked alms, but Thy worshippers saw me and said, "He is strong and lazy, and he should not beg."

"Oh Lord, it is Thy will that my mother gave birth unto me, and now the earth offers me back to you before the Ending."

His expression then changed. He arose and his eyes now glittered in determination. He fashioned a thick and heavy stick from the branch of the tree, and pointed it toward the city, shouting, "I asked for bread with all the strength of my voice, and was refused. Now I shall obtain it by the strength of my muscles! I asked for bread in the name of mercy and love, but humanity did not heed. I shall take it now in the name of evil!"

The passing years rendered the youth a robber, killer, and destroyer of souls; he crushed all who opposed him; he amassed fabulous wealth with which he won himself over to those in power. He was admired by colleagues, envied by other thieves, and feared by the multitudes.

His riches and false position prevailed upon the Emir to appoint him deputy in that city—the sad process pursued by unwise governors. Thefts were then legalized; oppression was supported by authority; crushing of the weak became commonplace; the throngs curried and praised.

Thus does the first touch of humanity's selfishness make criminals of the humble, and make killers of the sons of peace; thus does the early greed of humanity grow and strike back at humanity a thousandfold!

The Playground of Life

ONE HOUR devoted to the pursuit of Beauty
And Love is worth a full century of glory
Given by the frightened weak to the strong.

From that hour comes man's Truth; and
During that century Truth sleeps between
The restless arms of disturbing dreams.

In that hour the soul sees for herself
The Natural Law, and for that century she
Imprisons herself behind the law of man;
And she is shackled with irons of oppression.

That hour was the inspiration of the Songs
Of Solomon, and that century was the blind
Power which destroyed the temple of Baalbek.

That hour was the birth of the Sermon on the
Mount, and that century wrecked the castles of
Palmyra and the tower of Babylon.

That hour was the Hegira of Mohammed, and that
Century forgot Allah, Golgotha, and Sinai.

One hour devoted to mourning and lamenting the
Stolen equality of the weak is nobler than a
Century filled with greed and usurpation.

It is at that hour when the heart is
Purified by flaming sorrow, and
Illuminated by the torch of Love.
And in the century, desires for Truth
Are buried in the bosom of the earth.
That hour is the root which must flourish.

That hour is the hour of contemplation,
The hour of meditation, the hour of
Prayer, and the hour of a new era of good.

And that century is a life of Nero spent
On self-investment taken solely from
Earthly substance.

This is life.
Portrayed on the stage for ages;
Recorded earthily for centuries;
Lived in strangeness for years;
Sung as a hymn for days;
Exalted for but an hour, but the
Hour is treasured by Eternity as a jewel.

Song of Fortune

Man and I are sweethearts.
He craves me and I long for him,
But alas! Between us has appeared
Arrival who brings us misery.
She is cruel and demanding,
Possessing empty lure.
Her name is Substance.
She follows wherever we go
And watches like a sentinel, bringing
Restlessness to my lover.

I ask for my beloved in the forest,
Under the trees, by the lakes.
I cannot find him, for Substance
Has spirited him to the clamorous
City and placed him on the throne
Of quaking, metal riches.

I call for him with the voice of
Knowledge and the song of Wisdom.
He does not hearken, for Substance
Has enticed him into the dungeon
Of selfishness, where avarice dwells.

I seek him in the field of Contentment,
But I am alone, for my rival has
Imprisoned him in the cave of gluttony
And greed, and locked him there
With painful chains of gold.

I call to him at dawn, when Nature smiles,
But he does not hear, for excess has
Laden his drugged eyes with sick slumber.

I beguile him at eventide, when Silence rules
And the flowers sleep. But he responds not,
For his fear over what the morrow will
Bring, shadows his thoughts.

He yearns to love me;
He asks for me in his own acts. But he
Will find me not except in God's acts.

He seeks me in the edifices of his glory
Which he has built upon the bones of others;
He whispers to me from among
His heaps of gold and silver;
But he will find me only by coming to
The house of Simplicity which God has built
At the brink of the stream of affection.

He desires to kiss me before his coffers,
But his lips will never touch mine except
In the richness of the pure breeze.

He asks me to share with him his
Fabulous wealth, but I will not forsake God's
Fortune; I will not cast off my cloak of beauty.

He seeks deceit for medium; I seek only
The medium of his heart.
He bruises his heart in his narrow cell;
I would enrich his heart with my love.

My beloved has learned how to shriek and
Cry for my enemy, Substance; I would
Teach him how to shed tears of affection

And mercy from the eyes of his soul
For all things,
And utter sighs of contentmert through
Those tears.

Man is my sweetheart;
I want to belong to him.

The City of the Dead

YESTERDAY I drew myself from the noisome throngs and proceeded into the field until I reached a knoll upon which Nature had spread her comely garments. Now I could breathe.

I looked back, and the city appeared with its magnificent mosques and stately residences, veiled by the smoke of the shops.

I commenced analyzing man's mission, but could conclude only that most of his life was identified with struggle and hardship. Then I tried not to ponder over what the sons of Adam had done, and centered my eyes on the field which is the throne of God's glory. In one secluded corner of the field I observed a burying ground surrounded by poplar trees.

There, between the city of the dead and the city of the living, I meditated. I thought of the eternal silence in the first and the endless sorrow in the second.

In the city of the living I found hope and despair, love and hatred, joy and sorrow, wealth and poverty, faith and infidelity.

In the city of the dead there is buried earth in earth that Nature converts, in the night's silence, into vegetation, and then into animal, and then into man. As my mind wandered in this fashion, I saw a procession moving slowly and reverently, accompanied by pieces of music that filled the sky with sad melody. It was an elaborate funeral. The dead was followed by the living who wept and lamented his going. As the cortege reached the place of interment the priests commenced praying and burning incense, and the musicians blowing and plucking their instruments, mourning the departed. Then the leaders came forward one after the other and recited their eulogies with fine choice of words.

At last the multitude departed, leaving the dead resting in a most spacious and beautiful vault, expertly designed in stone and iron, and surrounded by the most expensively-entwined wreaths of flowers.

The farewell-bidders returned to the city and I remained, watching them from a distance and speaking softly to myself while the sun was descending to the horizon and Nature was making her many preparations for slumber.

Then I saw two men laboring under the weight of a wooden casket, and behind them a shabby-appearing woman carrying an infant on her arms. Following last was a dog who, with heartbreaking eyes, stared first at the woman and then at the casket.

It was a poor funeral. This guest of Death left to cold society a miserable wife and an infant to share her sorrows, and a faithful dog whose heart knew of his companion's departure.

As they reached the burial place they deposited the casket into a ditch away from the tended shrubs and marble stones, and retreated after a few simple words to God. The dog made one last turn to look at his friend's grave as the small group disappeared behind the trees.

I looked at the city of the living and said to myself, "That place belongs to the few." Then I looked upon the trim city of the dead and said, "That place, too, belongs to the few. Oh Lord, where is the haven of all people?"

As I said this, I looked toward the clouds, mingled with the sun's longest and most beautiful golden rays. I heard a voice within me saying, "Over there!"

Song of the Rain

I AM dotted silver threads dropped from heaven
By the gods. Nature then takes me, to adorn
Her fields and valleys.

I am beautiful pearls, plucked from the
Crown of Ishtar by the daughter of Dawn
To embellish the gardens.

When I cry the hills laugh;
When I humble myself the flowers rejoice;
When I bow, all things are elated.

The field and the cloud are lovers
And between them I am a messenger of mercy.
I quench the thirst of the one;
I cure the ailment of the other.

The voice of thunder declares my arrival;
The rainbow announces my departure.

I am like earthly life, which begins at
The feet of the mad elements and ends
Under the upraised wings of death.

I emerge from the heart of the sea and
Soar with the breeze. When I see a field in
Need, I descend and embrace the flowers and
The trees in a million little ways.

I touch gently at the windows with my
Soft fingers, and my announcement is a
Welcome song. All can hear, but only
The sensitive can understand.

The heat in the air gives birth to me,
But in turn I kill it,
As woman overcomes man with
The strength she takes from him.

   •   •   •   •   •   •   •

I am the sigh of the sea;
The laughter of the field;
The tears of heaven.

So with love—
Sighs from the deep sea of affection;
Laughter from the colorful field of the spirit;
Tears from the endless heaven of memories.

The Widow and Her Son

Night fell over North Lebanon and snow was covering the villages surrounded by the Kadeesha Valley, giving the fields and prairies the appearance of a great sheet of parchment upon which the furious Nature was recording her many deeds. Men came home from the streets while silence engulfed the night.

In a lone house near those villages lived a woman who sat by her fireside spinning wool, and at her side was her only child, staring now at the fire and then at his mother.

A terrible roar of thunder shook the house and the little boy took fright. He threw his arms about his mother, seeking protection from Nature in her affection. She took him to her bosom and kissed him; then she sat him on her lap and said, "Do not fear, my son, for Nature is but comparing her great power to man's weakness. There is a Supreme Being beyond the falling snow and the heavy clouds and the blowing wind, and He knows the needs of the earth, for He made it; and He looks upon the weak with merciful eyes.

Be brave, my boy. Nature smiles in Spring and laughs in Summer and yawns in Autumn, but now she is weeping; and with her tears she waters life, hidden under the earth.

Sleep, my dear child; your father is viewing us from Eternity. The snow and thunder bring us closer to him at this time.

Sleep, my beloved, for this white blanket which makes us cold, keeps the seeds warm, and these war-like things will produce beautiful flowers when Nisan comes.

Thus, my child, man cannot reap love until after sad and revealing separation, and bitter patience, and desperate hardship. Sleep, my little boy; sweet dreams will

42

find your soul who is unafraid of the terrible darkness of night and the biting frost."

The little boy looked upon his mother with sleep-laden eyes and said, "Mother, my eyes are heavy, but I cannot go to sleep without saying my prayer."

The woman looked at his angelic face, her vision blurred by misted eyes, and said, "Repeat with me, my boy—'God, have mercy on the poor and protect them from the winter; warm their thin-clad bodies with Thy merciful hands; look upon the orphans who are sleeping in wretched houses, suffering from hunger and cold. Hear, oh Lord, the call of widows who are helpless and shivering with fear for their young. Open, oh Lord, the hearts of all humans, that they may see the misery of the weak. Have mercy upon the sufferers who knock on doors, and lead the wayfarers into warm places. Watch, oh Lord, over the little birds and protect the trees and fields from the anger of the storm; for Thou art merciful and full of love.'"

As Slumber captured the boy's spirit, his mother placed him in the bed and kissed his eyes with quivering lips. Then she went back and sat by the hearth, spinning the wool to make him raiment.

The Poet

HE IS a link between this and the coming world. He is
A pure spring from which all thirsty souls may drink.

He is a tree watered by the River of Beauty, bearing
Fruit which the hungry heart craves;
He is a nightingale, soothing the depressed
Spirit with his beautiful melodies;
He is a white cloud appearing over the horizon,
Ascending and growing until it fills the face of the sky.
Then it falls on the flowers in the Field of Life,
Opening their petals to admit the light.

He is an angel, sent by the goddess to
Preach the Deity's gospel;
He is a brilliant lamp, unconquered by darkness
And inextinguishable by the wind. It is filled with
Oil by Ishtar of Love, and lighted by Apollon of Music.

He is a solitary figure, robed in simplicity and
Kindness; He sits upon the lap of Nature to draw his
Inspiration, and stays up in the silence of the night,
Awaiting the descending of the spirit.

He is a sower who sows the seeds of his heart in the
Prairies of affection, and humanity reaps the
Harvest for her nourishment.

This is the poet—whom the people ignore in this life,
And who is recognized only after he bids the earthly
World farewell and returns to his arbor in heaven.

This is the poet—who asks naught of
Humanity but a smile.
This is the poet—whose spirits ascends and

Fills the firmament with beautiful sayings;
Yet the people deny themselves his radiance.

Until when shall the people remain asleep?
Until when shall they continue to glorify those
Who attained greatness by moments of advantage?
How long shall they ignore those who enable
Them to see the beauty of their spirit,
Symbol of peace and love?
Until when shall human beings honor the dead
And forget the living, who spend their lives
Encircled in misery, and who consume themselves
Like burning candles to illuminate the way
For the ignorant and lead them into the path of light

Poet, you are the life of this life, and you have
Triumphed over the ages despite their severity.

Poet, you will one day rule the hearts, and
Therefore, your kingdom has no ending.
Poet, examine your crown of thorns; you will
Find concealed in it a budding wreath of laurel.

Song of the Soul

In the depth of my soul there is
A wordless song—a song that lives
In the seed of my heart.
It refuses to melt with ink on
Parchment; it engulfs my affection
In a transparent cloak and flows,
But not upon my lips.

How can I sigh it? I fear it may
Mingle with earthly ether;
To whom shall I sing it? It dwells
In the house of my soul, in fear of
Harsh ears.

When I look into my inner eyes
I see the shadow of its shadow;
When I touch my fingertips
I feel its vibrations.
The deeds of my hands heed its
Presence as a lake must reflect
The glittering stars; my tears
Reveal it, as bright drops of dew
Reveal the secret of a withering rose.

It is a song composed by contemplation,
And published by silence,
And shunned by clamor,
And folded by truth,
And repeated by dreams,
And understood by love,
And hidden by awakening,
And sung by the soul.

It is the song of love;
What Cain or Esau could sing it?

It is more fragrant than jasmine;
What voice could enslave it?

It is heartbound, as a virgin's secret;
What strings could quiver it?
Who dares unite the roar of the sea
And the singing of the nightingale?
Who dares compare the shrieking tempest
To the sigh of an infant?
Who dares speak aloud the words
Intended for the heart to speak?
What human dares sing in voice
The song of God?

Laughter and Tears

As THE Sun withdrew his rays from the garden, and the moon threw cushioned beams upon the flowers, I sat under the trees pondering upon the phenomena of the atmosphere, looking through the branches at the strewn stars which glittered like chips of silver upon a blue carpet; and I could hear from a distance the agitated murmur of the rivulet singing its way briskly into the valley.

When the birds took shelter among the boughs, and the flowers folded their petals, and tremendous silence descended, I heard a rustle of feet through the grass. I took heed and saw a young couple approaching my arbor. They sat under a tree where I could see them without being seen.

After he looked about in every direction, I heard the young man saying, "Sit by me, my beloved, and listen to my heart; smile, for your happiness is a symbol of our future; be merry, for the sparkling days rejoice with us.

My soul is warning me of the doubt in your heart, for doubt in love is a sin.

Soon you will be the owner of this vast land, lighted by this beautiful moon; soon you will be the mistress of my palace, and all the servants and maids will obey your commands.

Smile, my beloved, like the gold smiles from my father's coffers.

My heart refuses to deny you its secret. Twelve months of comfort and travel await us; for a year we will spend my father's gold at the blue lakes of Switzerland, and viewing the edifices of Italy and Egypt, and resting under the Holy Cedars of Lebanon; you will meet the princesses who will envy you for your jewels and clothes.

48

All these things I will do for you; will you be satisfied?"

In a little while I saw them walking and stepping on flowers as the rich step upon the hearts of the poor. As they disappeared from my sight, I commenced to make comparison between love and money, and to analyze their position in my heart.

Money! The source of insincere love; the spring of false light and fortune; the well of poisoned water; the desperation of old age!

I was still wandering in the vast desert of contemplation when a forlorn and specter-like couple passed by me and sat on the grass; a young man and a young woman who had left their farming shacks in the nearby fields for this cool and solitary place.

After a few moments of complete silence, I heard the following words uttered with sighs from weather-bitten lips, "Shed not tears, my beloved; love that opens our eyes and enslaves our hearts can give us the blessings of patience. Be consoled in our delay, for we have taken an oath and entered Love's shrine; for our love will ever grow in adversity; for it is in Love's name that we are suffering the obstacles of poverty and the sharpness of misery and the emptiness of separation. I shall attack these hardships until I triumph and place in your hands a strength that will help over all things to complete the journey of life.

Love—which is God—will consider our sighs and tears as incense burned at His altar and He will reward us with fortitude. Good-bye, my beloved; I must leave before the heartening moon vanishes."

A pure voice, combined of the consuming flame of love, and the hopeless bitterness of longing and the resolved sweetness of patience, said, "Good-bye, my beloved."

They separated, and the elegy to their union was smothered by the wails of my crying heart.

I looked upon slumbering Nature, and with deep reflection discovered the reality of a vast and infinite thing—something no power could demand, influence acquire, or riches purchase. Nor could it be effaced by the tears of time or deadened by sorrow; a thing which cannot be discovered by the blue lakes of Switzerland or the beautiful edifices of Italy.

It is something that gathers strength with patience, grows despite obstacles, warms in winter, flourishes in spring, casts a breeze in summer, and bears fruit in autumn—I found Love.

Song of the Flower

I AM A KIND word uttered and repeated
By the voice of Nature;
I am a star fallen from the
Blue tent upon the green carpet.
I am the daughter of the elements
With whom Winter conceived;
To whom Spring gave birth; I was
Reared in the lap of Summer and I
Slept in the bed of Autumn.

At dawn I unite with the breeze
To announce the coming of light;
At eventide I join the birds
In bidding the light farewell.

The plains are decorated with
My beautiful colors, and the air
Is scented with my fragrance.

As I embrace Slumber the eyes of
Night watch over me, and as I
Awaken I stare at the sun, which is
The only eye of the day.

I drink dew for wine, and harken to
The voices of the birds, and dance
To the rhythmic swaying of the grass.

I am the lover's gift; I am the wedding wreath;
I am the memory of a moment of happiness;
I am the last gift of the living to the dead;
I am a part of joy and a part of sorrow.

But I look up high to see only the light,
And never look down to see my shadow.
This is wisdom which man must learn.

Vision

THERE IN THE middle of the field, by the side of a crystalline stream, I saw a bird-cage whose rods and hinges were fashioned by an expert's hands. In one corner lay a dead bird, and in another were two basins—one empty of water and the other of seeds. I stood there reverently, as if the lifeless bird and the murmur of the water were worthy of deep silence and respect—something worthy of examination and meditation by the heart and conscience.

As I engrossed myself in view and thought, I found that the poor creature had died of thirst beside a stream of water, and of hunger in the midst of a rich field, cradle of life; like a rich man locked inside his iron safe, perishing from hunger amid heaps of gold.

Before my eyes I saw the cage turned suddenly into a human skeleton, and the dead bird into a man's heart which was bleeding from a deep wound that looked like the lips of a sorrowing woman. A voice came from that wound saying, "I am the human heart, prisoner of substance and victim of earthly laws.

In God's field of Beauty, at the edge of the stream of life, I was imprisoned in the cage of laws made by man.

In the center of beautiful Creation I died neglected because I was kept from enjoying the freedom of God's bounty.

Every thing of beauty that awakens my love and desire is a disgrace, according to man's conceptions; everything of goodness that I crave is but naught, according to his judgment.

I am the lost human heart, imprisoned in the foul dungeon of man's dictates, tied with chains of earthly authority, dead and forgotten by laughing humanity whose tongue is tied and whose eyes are empty of visible tears."

53

All these words I heard, and I saw them emerging with a stream of ever-thinning blood from that wounded heart.

More was said, but my misted eyes and crying soul prevented further sight or hearing.

The Victors

BY THE EDGE of the lake, in the shade of cypress and willow trees, a farmer's son sat contemplating the calm and silent water.

He had been reared close to Nature, where everything bespeaks love—the branches embrace, the flowers tempt, the grass moves gracefully, the birds call to each other, and God preaches His gospel in many voices.

He was a youth, and yestereve he had observed a young maiden sitting with other damsels at this lake. He had fallen in love with her instantly and completely.

Now, on learning that she was the Emir's daughter, he blamed his heart for having opened. But blaming never diverts the heart from its purpose, and loneliness deflects not the soul from the truth. A man between his heart and his soul is like a tender branch between the north and south winds.

As he looked about through his misted eyes, he saw the simple violets growing close by the noble jasmine; he saw the humming-bird upon the same tree with the robin. Yet the clamor of his heart insisted that the stately tree is hurt by the blades of grass encroaching at its roots.

He wept in his suffering, but like swift ghosts the hours slipped away, and with a sigh full of sweetness and affection he said, "What I see here is love ridiculing me, converting my hopes into pity, and my desires into disgrace.

The love which I worship elevates my heart into the Emir's palace and lowers it into the farmer's hut; it leads solidly into my spirit a young woman surrounded by admirers, served by slaves and protected by the strength of her ancestry.

I am following you, oh Love!

What do you seek of me? I have walked with you

upon the flaming path, and when I opened my eyes, I saw naught but darkness. My lips quivered, but you let them speak only words of misery. Love, you have made my heart hungry for the sweetness of your presence, for I am weak and you are strong; why are you struggling with me?

I am innocent and you are just. Why do you oppress me?

You are my very being. Why do you injure me?

You are my strength. Why do you weaken me?

You are my guide. Why do you desert me in this wilderness?

I am at the feet of your mercy, and will follow no path but your own. It is your will and my obedience that make my soul happy, shaded in the open field by your wings.

The brooks hurry to their lover, the sea.

The flowers smile at their sweetheart, the sun.

The clouds descend to their suitor, the valley.

I am unheard by the brooks, unseen by the flowers, unknown to the clouds.

I am solitary in my love, far even from the one who accepts me not as a soldier in her father's guard, nor as a servant in her palace; she knows not of my very existence."

He became silent for a moment, as if wanting to learn the language of the murmur of the brook and the rustle of the flowers. Then he said, "And you, whose name I fear to call, secluded behind the shades of glory, and the walls of dignity, and the doors of iron—where can we meet but in Eternity? There, equality rules and self-being may be expressed.

You have taken possession of my heart which Love has blessed, and enslaved my soul which God has honored.

Yesterday I was carefree, living peacefully in these fields; yet today I am a prisoner of my absent heart.

When I saw you, Oh Beautiful, I understood the purpose for my coming into this world.

When I discovered that you are a princess, and I

looked upon my poverty, I learned that God possesses a secret unrevealed to man; that a secret path leads the spirit to places where love may forget the customs of the earth. When I looked at your eyes, I knew that this path leads to a paradise whose door is the human heart.

And as I compared your station to my wretchedness, I saw them as a giant and a dwarf locked in struggle, and I realized that this earth is no more my homeland.

Yesterday I saw you surrounded by virgins, like a rose amidst the myrtles, and I believed that the vision of my dreams had descended from heaven to me. But with the knowledge of your father's glory, I discovered that the hands, picking the rose, would suffer bleeding from hidden thorns, seen too late, and what my dreams had gathered would be lost on awakening."

The youth stood up and walked slowly and sadly toward a spring. He flung his face into his hands, and begged in despair, "Oh Death, come and take me, for the earth, whose thorns choke its roses, is not just; come and deliver me from this kingdom of differences in a world that dethrones love of its heavenly glory and replaces it with shallow dignity. Help me, oh Death, for Eternity is the only place. There I shall wait for my beloved."

At eventide he still wandered in body and in mind, and the sun had already withdrawn its rays from the fields. He sat in the small arbor in which the Emir's daughter had walked. He dropped his head to his chest as if to keep his heart from bursting.

At that moment a beautiful young woman appeared from behind the willow trees, her robes trailing over the green grass She stood by him and placed her soft hand upon his head As if in insanity he stared at her, not believing the picture o his eyes. She was the Emir's daughter!

He knelt as did Moses when he saw the flaming bush; he struggled to speak but found himself mute, substituting with tears.

The princess embraced him and printed a kiss upon his lips; she dried his tears with her soft cheeks, and with a voice more soothing than the sounds of music, she spoke, "You appeared in my dream of sadness, and your image ended my loneliness. You are the companion of my lost soul, and you are my other half from which I was torn when I came to this world.

I fled the palace to see you, and you are now with me. Do not be frightened for me; I have left my father's glory to follow you into the distant land and drink the cup of life and death with you. Come, let us leave this place for another, where this earth cannot be with us."

The couple walked side by side in the midst of the trees, until hidden by the obscurity of night. And as they walked, they were enveloped in an increasing glow of light. Now they were unafraid of the darkness, fearless of the Emir's punishment.

•   •   •   •   •   •   •

There, in the farthest portion of the land, the Emir's soldiers found the skeletons of two humans. About the neck of one was tied a gold locket, and by their side, a great stone. Upon each was inscribed:

> What Death takes away
> No man can restore;
> What Heaven has blessed
> No man can punish;
> What Love has joined
> No man can divide;
> What Eternity has willed
> No man can alter.

Song of Love

I AM THE lover's eyes, and the spirit's
Wine, and the heart's nourishment.
I am a rose. My heart opens at dawn and
The virgin kisses me and places me
Upon her breast.

I am the house of true fortune, and the
Origin of pleasure, and the beginning
Of peace and tranquility. I am the gentle
Smile upon the lips of beauty. When youth
Overtakes me he forgets his toil, and his
Whole life becomes reality of sweet dreams.

I am the poet's elation,
And the artist's revelation,
And the musician's inspiration.

I am a sacred shrine in the heart of a
Child, adored by a merciful mother.
I appear to a heart's cry; I shun a demand;
My fullness pursues the heart's desire;
It shuns the empty claim of the voice.

I appeared to Adam through Eve
And exile was his lot;
Yet I revealed myself to Solomon, and
He drew wisdom from my presence.

I smiled at Helena and she destroyed Tarwada;
Yet I crowned Cleopatra and peace dominated
The Valley of the Nile.

I am like the ages—building today
And destroying tomorrow;

I am like a god, who creates and ruin
I am sweeter than a violet's sigh;
I am more violent than a raging tempest.

Gifts alone do not entice me;
Parting does not discourage me;
Poverty does not chase me;
Jealousy does not prove my awareness;
Madness does not evidence my presence.

Oh seekers, I am Truth, beseeching Truth;
And your Truth in seeking and receiving
And protecting me shall determine my
Behavior.

Two Wishes

IN THE silence of the night Death descended from God toward the earth. He hovered above a city and pierced the dwellings with his eyes. He saw the spirits floating on wings of dreams, and the people who were surrendered to the mercy of Slumber.

When the moon fell below the horizon and the city became black, Death walked silently among the houses —careful to touch nothing—until he reached a palace. He entered through the bolted gates undisturbed, and stood by the rich man's bed; and as Death touched his forehead, the sleeper's eyes opened, showing great fright.

When he saw the specter, he summoned a voice mingled with fear and anger, and said, "Go away, oh horrible dream; leave me, you dreadful ghost. Who are you? How did you enter this place? What do you want? Leave this place at once, for I am the lord of the house and will call my slaves and guards, and order them to kill you!"

Then Death spoke, softly but with smoldering thunder, "I am Death. Stand and bow!"

The man responded, "What do you want? Why have you come here when I have not yet finished my affairs? What seek you from strength such as mine? Go to the weak man, and take him away!

I loathe the sight of your bloody paws and hollow face, and my eyes take sick at your horrible ribbed wings and cadaverous body."

After a quiet moment of fearful realization he added, "No, no, oh merciful Death! Mind not my talk, for fear reveals what the heart forbids.

Take a bushelful of my gold, or a handful of my slaves' souls, but leave me. I have accounts with Life requiring settling; I have due from the people much gold;

61

my ships have not reached the harbor; my wheat has not been harvested. Take anything you demand, but spare my life. Death, I own harems of supernatural beauty; your choice is my gift to you. Give heed, Death —I have but one child, and I love him dearly for he is my only joy in this life. I offer supreme sacrifice—take him, but spare me!"

Death murmured, "You are not rich, but pitifully poor." Then Death took the hand of that earthly slave, removed his reality, and gave to the angels the heavy task of correction.

And Death walked slowly amidst the dwellings of the poor until he reached the most miserable he could find. He entered and approached a bed upon which a youth slept fitfully. Death touched his eyes; the lad sprang up as he saw Death standing by, and, with a voice full of love and hope he said, "Here I am, my beautiful Death. Accept my soul, for you are the hope of my dreams. Be their accomplishment! Embrace me, oh beloved Death! You are merciful; do not leave me. You are God's messenger; deliver me to Him. You are the right hand of Truth and the heart of Kindness; do not neglect me.

I have begged for you many times, but you did not come; I have sought you, but you avoided me; I called out to you, but you listened not. You hear me now— embrace my soul, beloved Death!"

Death placed his softened hand upon the trembling lips, removed all reality, and enfolded it beneath his wings for secure conduct. And returning to the sky, Death looked back and whispered his warning:

"Only those return to Eternity
Who on earth seek out Eternity."

Song of Man

I WAS HERE from the moment of the
Beginning, and here I am still. And
I shall remain here until the end
Of the world, for there is no
Ending to my grief-stricken being.

I roamed the infinite sky, and
Soared in the ideal world, and
Floated through the firmament. But
Here I am, prisoner of measurement.

I heard the teachings of Confucius;
I listened to Brahma's wisdom;
I sat by Buddha under the Tree of Knowledge.
Yet here am I, existing with ignorance
And heresy.

I was on Sinai when Jehovah approached Moses;
I saw the Nazarene's miracles at the Jordan;
I was in Medina when Mohammed visited.
Yet here I am, prisoner of bewilderment.

Then I witnessed the might of Babylon;
I learned of the glory of Egypt;
I viewed the warring greatness of Rome.
Yet my earlier teachings showed the
Weakness and sorrow of those achievements.

I conversed with the magicians of Ain Dour;
I debated with the priests of Assyria;
I gleaned depth from the prophets of Palestine.
Yet, I am still seeking the truth.

I gathered wisdom from quiet India;
I probed the antiquity of Arabia;
I heard all that can be heard.
Yet, my heart is deaf and blind.

I suffered at the hands of despotic rulers;
I suffered slavery under insane invaders;
I suffered hunger imposed by tyranny;
Yet, I still possess some inner power
With which I struggle to greet each day.

My mind is filled, but my heart is empty;
My body is old, but my heart is an infant.
Perhaps in youth my heart will grow, but I
Pray to grow old and reach the moment of
My return to God. Only then will my heart fill!

I was here from the moment of the
Beginning, and here I am still. And
I shall remain here until the end
Of the world, for there is no
Ending to my grief-stricken being.

Yesterday and Today

THE GOLD-HOARDER walked in his palace park and with him walked his troubles. And over his head hovered worries as a vulture hovers over a carcass, until he reached a beautiful lake surrounded by magnificent marble statuary.

He sat there pondering the water which poured from the mouths of the statues like thoughts flowing freely from a lover's imagination, and contemplating heavily his palace which stood upon a knoll like a birth-mark upon the cheek of a maiden. His fancy revealed to him the pages of his life's drama which he read with falling tears that veiled his eyes and prevented him from viewing man's feeble additions to Nature.

He looked back with piercing regret to the images of his early life, woven into pattern by the gods, until he could no longer control his anguish. He said aloud, "Yesterday I was grazing my sheep in the green valley, enjoying my existence, sounding my flute, and holding my head high. Today I am a prisoner of greed. Gold leads into gold, then into restlessness, and finally into crushing misery.

Yesterday I was like a singing bird, soaring freely here and there in the fields. Today I am a slave to fickle wealth, society's rules, the city's customs, and purchased friends, pleasing the people by conforming to the strange and narrow laws of man. I was born to be free and enjoy the bounty of life, but I find myself like a beast of burden so heavily laden with gold that his back is breaking.

Where are the spacious plains, the singing brooks, the pure breeze, the closeness of Nature? Where is my deity? I have lost all! Naught remains save loneliness that saddens me, gold that ridicules me, slaves who curse to my back, and a palace that I have erected as a tomb for my happiness, and in whose greatness I have lost my heart.

Yesterday I roamed the prairies and the hills together with the Bedouin's daughter; Virtue was our companion, Love our delight, and the moon our guardian. Today I am among women with shallow beauty who sell themselves for gold and diamonds.

Yesterday I was carefree, sharing with the shepherds all the joy of life; eating, playing, working, singing, and dancing together to the music of the heart's truth. Today I find myself among the people like a frightened lamb among the wolves. As I walk in the roads, they gaze at me with hateful eyes and point at me with scorn and jealousy, and as I steal through the park I see frowning faces all about me.

Yesterday I was rich in happiness and today I am poor in gold.

Yesterday I was a happy shepherd looking upon my herd as a merciful king looks with pleasure upon his contented subjects. Today I am a slave standing before my wealth, my wealth which robbed me of the beauty of life I once knew.

Forgive me, my Judge! I did not know that riches would put my life in fragments and lead me into the dungeons of harshness and stupidity. What I thought was glory is naught but an eternal inferno."

He gathered himself wearily and walked slowly toward the palace, sighing and repeating, "Is this what people call wealth? Is this the god I am serving and worshipping? Is this what I seek of the earth? Why can I not trade it for one particle of contentment? Who would sell me one beautiful thought for a ton of gold? Who would give me one moment of love for a handful of gems? Who would grant me an eye that can see others' hearts, and take all my coffers in barter?"

As he reached the palace gates he turned and looked toward the city as Jeremiah gazed toward Jerusalem. He raised his arms in woeful lament and shouted, "Oh people of the noisome city, who are living in darkness, hastening toward misery, preaching falsehood, and
66

speaking with stupidity . . . until when shall you remain ignorant? Until when shall you abide in the filth of life and continue to desert its gardens? Why wear you tattered robes of narrowness while the silk raiment of Nature's beauty is fashioned for you? The lamp of wisdom is dimming; it is time to furnish it with oil. The house of true fortune is being destroyed; it is time to rebuild it and guard it. The thieves of ignorance have stolen the treasure of your peace; it is time to retake it!"

At that moment a poor man stood before him and stretched forth his hand for alms. As he looked at the beggar, his lips parted, his eyes brightened with a softness, and his face radiated kindness. It was as if the yesterday he had lamented by the lake had come to greet him. He embraced the pauper with affection and filled his hand with gold, and with a voice sincere with the sweetness of love he said, "Come back tomorrow and bring with you your fellow sufferers. All your possessions will be restored."

He entered his palace saying, "Everything in life is good; even gold, for it teaches a lesson. Money is like a stringed instrument; he who does not know how to use it properly will hear only discordant music. Money is like love; it kills slowly and painfully the one who withholds it, and it enlivens the other who turns it upon his fellow men."

Before the Throne of Beauty

ONE HEAVY day I ran away from the grim face of society and the dizzying clamor of the city and directed my weary steps to the spacious valley. I pursued the beckoning course of the rivulet and the musical sounds of the birds until I reached a lonely spot where the flowing branches of the trees prevented the sun from touching the earth.

I stood there, and it was entertaining to my soul—my thirsty soul who had seen naught but the mirage of life instead of its sweetness.

I was engrossed deeply in thought and my spirits were sailing the firmament when a Houri, wearing a sprig of grapevine that covered part of her naked body, and a wreath of poppies about her golden hair, suddenly appeared to me. As she realized my astonishment, she greeted me saying, "Fear me not; I am the Nymph of the Jungle."

"How can beauty like yours be committed to live in this place? Please tell me who you are and whence you come?" I asked. She sat gracefully on the green grass and responded, "I am the symbol of Nature! I am the Ever-Virgin your forefathers worshipped, and to my honor they erected shrines and temples at Baalbek and Djabeil." And I dared say, "But those temples and shrines were laid waste and the bones of my adoring ancestors became a part of the earth; nothing was left to commemorate their goddess save a pitiful few and forgotten pages in the book of history."

She replied, "Some goddesses live in the lives of their worshippers and die in their death, while some live an eternal and infinite life. My life is sustained by the world of Beauty which you will see wherever you rest your eyes, and this Beauty is Nature itself; it is the beginning of the Shepherd's joy among the hills, and a villager's happiness in the fields, and the pleasure of the awe-filled tribes between the mountains and the plains. This Beauty promotes the wise into the throne of Truth."

Then I said, "Beauty is a terrible power!" And she retorted, "Human beings fear all things, even yourselves. You fear heaven, the source of spiritual peace; you fear Nature, the haven of rest and tranquility; you fear the God of goddess and accuse him of anger, while he is full of love and mercy."

After a deep silence, mingled with sweet dreams, I asked, "Speak to me of that Beauty which the people interpret and define, each one according to his own conception; I have seen her honored and worshipped in different ways and manners."

She answered, "Beauty is that which attracts your soul, and that which loves to give and not to receive. When you meet Beauty, you feel that the hands deep within your inner self are stretched forth to bring her into the domain of your heart. It is a magnificence combined of sorrow and joy; it is the Unseen which you see, and the Vague which you understand, and the Mute which you hear—it is the Holy of Holies that begins in yourself and ends vastly beyond your earthly imagination."

Then the Nymph of the Jungle approached me and laid her scented hand upon my eyes. And as she withdrew, I found me alone in the valley. When I returned to the city, whose turbulence no longer vexed me, I repeated her words:

"Beauty is that which attracts your soul,
And that which loves to give and not to receive."

Leave Me, My Blamer

LEAVE me, my blamer,
For the sake of the love
Which unites your soul with
That of your beloved one;
For the sake of that which
Joins spirit with mother's
Affection, and ties your
Heart with filial love. Go,
And leave me to my own
Weeping heart.

Let me sail in the ocean of
My dreams; wait until Tomorrow
Comes, for Tomorrow is free to
Do with me as he wishes. Your
Flaying is naught but shadow
That walks with the spirit to
The tomb of abashment, and shows
Her the cold, solid earth.

I have a little heart within me
And I like to bring him out of
His prison and carry him on the
Palm of my hand to examine him
In depth and extract his secret.
Aim not your arrows at him, lest
He take fright and vanish ere he
Pours the secret's blood as a
Sacrifice at the altar of his
Own faith, given him by Deity
When He fashioned him of Love and Beauty.

The sun is rising and the nightingale
Is singing, and the myrtle is

Breathing its fragrance into space.
I want to free myself from the
Quilted slumber of wrong. Do not
Detain me, my blamer!

Cavil me not by mention of the
Lions of the forest or the
Snakes of the valley, for
My soul knows no fear of earth and
Accepts no warning of evil before
Evil comes.

Advise me not, my blamer, for
Calamities have opened my heart and
Tears have cleansed my eyes, and
Errors have taught me the language
Of the hearts.

Talk not of banishment, for Conscience
Is my judge and he will justify me
And protect me if I am innocent, and
Will deny me of life if I am a criminal.

Love's procession is moving;
Beauty is waving her banner;
Youth is sounding the trumpet of joy;
Disturb not my contrition, my blamer.
Let me walk, for the path is rich
With roses and mint, and the air
Is scented with cleanliness.

Relate not the tales of wealth and
Greatness, for my soul is rich
With bounty and great with God's glory.

Speak not of peoples and laws and
Kingdoms, for the whole earth is
My birthplace and all humans are
My brothers.

Go from me, for you are taking away
Light-giving repentance and bringing
Needless words.

A Lover's Call

WHERE are you, my beloved? Are you in that little
Paradise, watering the flowers who look upon you
As infants look upon the breast of their mothers?

Or are you in your chamber where the shrine of
Virtue has been placed in your honor, and upon
Which you offer my heart and soul as sacrifice?

Or amongst the books, seeking human knowledge,
While you are replete with heavenly wisdom?
Oh companion of my soul, where are you? Are you
Praying in the temple? Or calling Nature in the
Field, haven of your dreams?

Are you in the huts of the poor, consoling the
Broken-hearted with the sweetness of your soul, and
Filling their hands with your bounty?
You are God's spirit everywhere;
You are stronger than the ages.

Do you have memory of the day we met, when the halo
of
Your spirit surrounded us, and the Angels of Love
Floated about, singing the praise of the soul's deeds?

Do you recollect our sitting in the shade of the
Branches, sheltering ourselves from Humanity, as the
ribs
Protect the divine secret of the heart from injury?

Remember you the trails and forest we walked, with
hands
Joined, and our heads leaning against each other, as if
We were hiding ourselves within ourselves?

Recall you the hour I bade you farewell,
And the Miriamite kiss you placed on my lips?
That kiss taught me that joining of lips in Love
Reveals heavenly secret which the tongue cannot utter!
That kiss was introduction to a great sigh,
Like the Almighty's breath that turned earth into man.

That sigh led my way into the spiritual world,
Announcing the glory of my soul; and there
It shall perpetuate until again we meet.

I remember when you kissed me and kissed me,
With tears coursing your cheeks, and you said,
"Earthly bodies must often separate for earthly purpose,
And must live apart impelled by worldly intent.

But the spirit remains joined safely in the hands of
Love, until death arrives and takes joined souls to God.

Go, my beloved; Life has chosen you her delegate;
Obey her, for she is Beauty who offers to her follower
The cup of the sweetness of life.
As for my own empty arms, your love shall remain my
Comforting groom; your memory, my Eternal wedding."

Where are you now, my other self? Are you awake in
The silence of the night? Let the clean breeze convey
To you my heart's every beat and affection.

Are you fondling my face in your memory? That image
Is no longer my own, for Sorrow has dropped his
Shadow on my happy countenance of the past.

Sobs have withered my eyes which reflected your beauty
And dried my lips which you sweetened with kisses.

Where are you, my beloved? Do you hear my weeping
From beyond the ocean? Do you understand my need?
Do you know the greatness of my patience?

Is there any spirit in the air capable of conveying
To you the breath of this dying youth? Is there any
Secret communication between angels that will carry to
You my complaint?

Where are you, my beautiful star? The obscurity of life
Has cast me upon its bosom; sorrow has conquered me.
Sail your smile into the air; it will reach and enliven me!
Breathe your fragrance into the air; it will sustain me!

Where are you, my beloved?
Oh, how great is Love!
And how little am I!

The Beauty of Death

Dedicated to M. E. H.

Part One—The Calling

LET ME sleep, for my soul is intoxicated with love, and
Let me rest, for my spirit has had its bounty of days
   and nights;
Light the candles and burn the incense around my bed,
   and
Scatter leaves of jasmine and roses over my body;
Embalm my hair with frankincense and sprinkle my
   feet with perfume,
And read what the hand of Death has written on my
   forehead.

Let me rest in the arms of Slumber, for my open eyes
   are tired;
Let the silver-stringed lyre quiver and soothe my spirit;
Weave from the harp and lute a veil around my wither-
   ing heart.
Sing of the past as you behold the dawn of hope in my
   eyes, for
Its magic meaning is a soft bed upon which my heart
   rests.

Dry your tears, my friends, and raise your heads as the
   flowers
Raise their crowns to greet the dawn.
Look at the bride of Death standing like a column of
   light
Between my bed and the infinite;
Hold your breath and listen with me to the beckoning
   rustle of
Her white wings.

Come close and bid me farewell; touch my eyes with
    smiling lips.
Let the children grasp my hands with soft and rosy
    fingers;
Let the aged place their veined hands upon my head
    and bless me;
Let the virgins come close and see the shadow of God
    in my eyes,
And hear the echo of His will racing with my breath.

Part Two—The Ascending

I have passed a mountain peak and my soul is soaring
    in the
Firmament of complete and unbound freedom;
I am far, far away, my companions, and the clouds are
Hiding the hills from my eyes.
The valleys are becoming flooded with an ocean of
    silence, and the
Hands of oblivion are engulfing the roads and the
    houses;
The prairies and fields are disappearing behind a white
    specter
That looks like the spring cloud, yellow as the candle-
    light
And red as the twilight.

The songs of the waves and the hymns of the streams
Are scattered, and the voices of the throngs reduced to
    silence;
And I can hear naught but the music of Eternity
In exact harmony with the spirit's desires.
I am cloaked in full whiteness;
I am in comfort; I am in peace.

Part Three—The Remains

Unwrap me from this white linen shroud and clothe me
With leaves of jasmine and lilies;
Take my body from the ivory casket and let it rest

77

Upon pillows of orange blossoms.
Lament me not, but sing songs of youth and joy;
Shed not tears upon me, but sing of harvest and the
  winepress;
Utter no sigh of agony, but draw upon my face with
  your
Finger the symbol of Love and Joy.
Disturb not the air's tranquility with chanting and
  requiems,
But let your hearts sing with me the song of Eternal
  Life;
Mourn me not with apparel of black,
But dress in color and rejoice with me;
Talk not of my departure with sighs in your hearts; close
Your eyes and you will see me with you forevermore.

Place me upon clusters of leaves and
Carry me upon your friendly shoulders and
Walk slowly to the deserted forest.
Take me not to the crowded burying ground lest my
  slumber
Be disrupted by the rattling of bones and skulls.
Carry me to the cypress woods and dig my grave where
  violets
And poppies grow not in the other's shadow;
Let my grave be deep so that the flood will not
Carry my bones to the open valley;
Let my grave be wide, so that the twilight shadows
Will come and sit by me.

Take from me all earthly raiment and place me deep
  in my
Mother Earth; and place me with care upon my mother's
  breast.
Cover me with soft earth, and let each handful be mixed
With seeds of jasmine, lilies, and myrtle; and when they
Grow above me and thrive on my body's element, they
  will
Breathe the fragrance of my heart into space;

And reveal even to the sun the secret of my peace;
And sail with the breeze and comfort the wayfarer.

Leave me then, friends—leave me and depart on mute
feet,
As the silence walks in the deserted valley;
Leave me to God and disperse yourselves slowly, as the
almond
And apple blossoms disperse under the vibration of
Nisan's breeze.

Go back to the joy of your dwellings and you will find
there
That which Death cannot remove from you and me.
Leave this place, for what you see here is far away in
meaning
From the earthly world. Leave me.

The Palace and the Hut

Part One

As NIGHT fell and the lights glittered in the great house, the servants stood at the massive door awaiting the coming of the guests; and upon their velvet garments shone golden buttons.

The magnificent carriages drew into the palace park and the nobles entered, dressed in gorgeous raiment and decorated with jewels. The instruments filled the air with pleasant melodies while the dignitaries danced to the soothing music.

At midnight the finest and most palatable foods were served on a beautiful table embellished with all kinds of the rarest flowers. The feasters dined and drank abundantly, until the sequence of the wine began to play its part. At dawn the throng dispersed boisterously, after spending a long night of intoxication and gluttony which hurried their worn bodies into their deep beds with unnatural sleep.

Part Two

At eventide, a man attired in the dress of heavy work stood before the door of his small house and knocked at the door. As it opened, he entered and greeted the occupants in a cheerful manner, and then sat between his children who were playing at the fireplace. In a short time, his wife had the meal prepared and they sat at a wooden table consuming their food. After eating they gathered around the oil lamp and talked of the day's events. When early night had lapsed, all stood silently and surrendered themselves to the King of Slumber with a song of praise and a prayer of gratitude upon their lips.

80

A *Poet's Voice*

Part One

THE POWER of charity sows deep in my heart, and I reap and gather the wheat in bundles and give them to the hungry.

My soul gives life to the grapevine and I press its bunches and give the juice to the thirsty.

Heaven fills my lamp with oil and I place it at my window to direct the stranger through the dark.

I do all these things because I live in them; and if destiny should tie my hands and prevent me from so doing, then death would be my only desire. For I am a poet, and if I cannot give, I shall refuse to receive.

Humanity rages like a tempest, but I sigh in silence for I know the storm must pass away while a sigh goes to God.

Human kinds cling to earthly things, but I seek ever to embrace the torch of love so it will purify me by its fire and sear inhumanity from my heart.

Substantial things deaden a man without suffering; love awakens him with enlivening pains.

Humans are divided into different clans and tribes, and belong to countries and towns. But I find myself a stranger to all communities and belong to no settlement. The universe is my country and the human family is my tribe.

Men are weak, and it is sad that they divide amongst themselves. The world is narrow and it is unwise to cleave it into kingdoms, empires, and provinces.

Human kinds unite themselves only to destroy the temples of soul, and they join hands to build edifices for earthly bodies. I stand alone listening to the voice of hope in my deep self saying, "As love enlivens a man's heart with pain, so ignorance teaches him the way to

81

knowledge." Pain and ignorance lead to great joy and knowledge because the Supreme Being has created nothing vain under the sun.

Part Two

I have a yearning for my beautiful country, and I love its people because of their misery. But if my people rose, stimulated by plunder and motivated by what they call "patriotic spirit" to murder, and invaded my neighbor's country, then upon the committing of any human atrocity I would hate my people and my country.

I sing the praise of my birthplace and long to see the home of my childhood; but if the people in that home refused to shelter and feed the needy wayfarer, I would convert my praise into eulogy and my longing into forgetfulness. My inner voice would say, "The house that does not comfort the needy is worthy of naught but destruction."

I love my native village with some of my love for my country; and I love my country with part of my love for the earth, all of which is my country; and I love the earth with all of myself because it is the haven of humanity, the manifest spirit of God.

Humanity is the spirit of the Supreme Being on earth, and that humanity is standing amidst ruins, hiding its nakedness behind tattered rags, shedding tears upon hollow cheeks, and calling for its children with pitiful voice. But the children are busy singing their clan's anthem; they are busy sharpening the swords and cannot hear the cry of their mothers.

Humanity appeals to its people but they listen not. Were one to listen, and console a mother by wiping her tears, others would say, "He is weak, affected by sentiment."

Humanity is the spirit of the Supreme Being on earth, and that Supreme Being preaches love and good-will. But the people ridicule such teachings. The Nazarene Jesus listened, and crucifixion was his lot; Socrates heard the voice and followed it, and he too fell victim in body.

82

The followers of The Nazarene and Socrates are the followers of Deity, and since people will not kill them, they deride them, saying, "Ridicule is more bitter than killing."

Jerusalem could not kill The Nazarene, nor Athens Socrates; they are living yet and shall live eternally. Ridicule cannot triumph over the followers of Deity. They live and grow forever.

Part Three

Thou art my brother because you are a human, and we both are sons of one Holy Spirit; we are equal and made of the same earth.

You are here as my companion along the path of life, and my aid in understanding the meaning of hidden Truth. You are a human, and, that fact sufficing, I love you as a brother. You may speak of me as you choose, for Tomorrow shall take you away and will use your talk as evidence for his judgment, and you shall receive justice.

You may deprive me of whatever I possess, for my greed instigated the amassing of wealth and you are entitled to my lot if it will satisfy you.

You may do unto me whatever you wish, but you shall not be able to touch my Truth.

You may shed my blood and burn my body, but you cannot kill or hurt my spirit.

You may tie my hands with chains and my feet with shackles, and put me in the dark prison, but you shall not enslave my thinking, for it is free, like the breeze in the spacious sky.

You are my brother and I love you. I love you worshiping in your church, kneeling in your temple, and praying in your mosque. You and I and all are children of one religion, for the varied paths of religion are but the fingers of the loving hand of the Supreme Being, extended to all, offering completeness of spirit to all, anxious to receive all.

I love you for your Truth, derived from your knowledge; that Truth which I cannot see because of my ignorance. But I respect it as a divine thing, for it is the deed of the spirit. Your Truth shall meet my Truth in the coming world and blend together like the fragrance of flowers and become one whole and eternal Truth, perpetuating and living in the eternity of Love and Beauty.

I love you because you are weak before the strong oppressor, and poor before the greedy rich. For these reasons I shed tears and comfort you; and from behind my tears I see you embraced in the arms of Justice, smiling and forgiving your persecutors. You are my brother and I love you.

Part Four

You are my brother, but why are you quarreling with me? Why do you invade my country and try to subjugate me for the sake of pleasing those who are seeking glory and authority?

Why do you leave your wife and children and follow Death to the distant land for the sake of those who buy glory with your blood, and high honor with your mother's tears?

Is it an honor for a man to kill his brother man? If you deem it an honor, let it be an act of worship, and erect a temple to Cain who slew his brother Abel.

Is self-preservation the first law of Nature? Why, then, does Greed urge you to self-sacrifice in order only to achieve his aim in hurting your brothers? Beware, my brother, of the leader who says, "Love of existence obliges us to deprive the people of their rights!" I say unto you but this: protecting others' rights is the noblest and most beautiful human act; if my existence requires that I kill others, then death is more honorable to me, and if I cannot find someone to kill me for the protection of my honor, I will not hesitate to take my life by my own hands for the sake of Eternity before Eternity comes.

Selfishness, my brother, is the cause of blind superiority, and superiority creates clanship, and clanship

84

creates authority which leads to discord and subjugation,

The soul believes in the power of knowledge and justice over dark ignorance; it denies the authority that supplies the swords to defend and strengthen ignorance and oppression—that authority which destroyed Babylon and shook the foundation of Jerusalem and left Rome in ruins. It is that which made people call criminals great men; made writers respect their names; made historians relate the stories of their inhumanity in manner of praise.

The only authority I obey is the knowledge of guarding and acquiescing in the Natural Law of Justice.

What justice does authority display when it kills the killer? When it imprisons the robber? When it descends on a neighboring country and slays its people? What does justice think of the authority under which a killer punishes the one who kills, and a thief sentences the one who steals?

You are my brother, and I love you; and Love is justice with its full intensity and dignity. If justice did not support my love for you, regardless of your tribe and community, I would be a deceiver concealing the ugliness of selfishness behind the outer garment of pure love.

Conclusion

My soul is my friend who consoles me in misery and distress of life. He who does not befriend his soul is an enemy of humanity, and he who does not find human guidance within himself will perish desperately. Life emerges from within, and derives not from environs.

I came to say a word and I shall say it now. But if death prevents its uttering, it will be said by Tomorrow, for Tomorrow never leaves a secret in the book of Eternity.

I came to live in the glory of Love and the light of Beauty, which are the reflections of God. I am here living, and the people are unable to exile me from the domain of life for they know I will live in death. If they pluck my eyes I will hearken to the murmurs of Love and the songs of Beauty.

If they close my ears I will enjoy the touch of the breeze mixed with the incense of Love and the fragrance of Beauty.

If they place me in vacuum, I will live together with my soul, the child of Love and Beauty.

I came here to be for all and with all, and what I do today in my solitude will be echoed by Tomorrow to the people.

What I say now with one heart will be said tomorrow by many hearts.

The Bride's Bed *

THE BRIDE and bridegroom, preceded by candle carriers and followed by priests and friends, left the temple accompanied by young men and women who walked by their sides singing and filling the firmament with beautiful and happy melodies.

As the procession reached the bridegroom's residence, the newly wed couple took high seats in the spacious room, and the celebrants seated themselves upon the silken cushions and velvet divans until the place became crowded with multitudes of well wishers. The servants set the tables, and the feasters commenced drinking to the health of the bride and bridegroom, while the musicians were soothing the spirits with their stringed instruments. One could hear the ringing and rattling of the drinking cups in unison with the sound of tambourines. The maidens began to dance gracefully and twist their flexible bodies to the melodies of the music, while the onlookers watched cheerfully and drank more and more wine.

In a few hours the scene was converted from a gay and pleasant wedding celebration into a coarse and profane orgy of drunkenness. Here is a young man pouring out all of his heart's sentiment and revealing his momentary, questionable love to an attractive maiden. And there is another youth endeavoring to converse with a woman, and having difficulty in bringing back to his wine-drugged memory the beautiful expressions he sought. Now and then, you hear an elderly man urging the musicians to repeat a certain song that reminded him of his youthful days. In this group a woman is flirting

* This incident occurred in North Lebanon in the latter part of the nineteenth century and it was conveyed to me by a person who was related to one of the principals in this story, and who attended the function described. [KAHLIL GIBRAN]

87

with a man who, in turn, is looking passionately at her rival. In that corner, a grey-haired woman is watching the maidens smilingly, trying to select a wife for her only son. By the window stands a married woman who affords herself this opportunity to make plans with her lover while her husband is busy drinking. It seemed that all were reaping the fruit of the present and forgetting the past and the future.

All this was taking place while the beautiful bride was watching them with sorrowful eyes. She felt like a miserable prisoner behind the iron bars of a prison, and frequently she glanced across the room toward a young man who was sitting alone and quietly, like a wounded bird left behind by the flock. His arms were folded across his bosom as if he were trying to keep his heart from bursting. He was gazing at something invisible in the sky of the room and seemed to be completely lost in a world of darkness.

Midnight came, and the exultation of the throng mounted higher until it assumed the aspects of unleashed madness, for the minds were free and the tongues were uncontrolled.

The bridegroom, who was an elderly man, already drunk, left the bride to herself and circulated amidst the guests, drinking with the feasters and adding fuel to the flames of his intoxication.

Responding to the bride's signal, a maiden came and sat close by her side, whereupon the bride turned around and looked in every direction before she whispered with a trembling voice, "I beg you, my companion, and appeal to you in the name of our friendship and everything that is dear to you in this world, to go now and tell Saleem to join me in the garden under the willow tree. Please, Susan, beg him for me and ask him to grant my request; remind him of our past and tell him that I will die if I do not see him. Tell him that I must confess my sins to him and ask him to forgive me; tell him that I want to pour out all my heart's secrets before him. Hurry, and do not fear."

Susan dispatched the bride's message with sincerity;

88

Saleem looked at her as a thirsty man looks at a brook far off and he quietly said, "I will wait for her in the garden under the willow tree." He left the house, and a few minutes passed before the bride followed him, stealing her way between the drunken revelers. As she reached the garden, she looked to the rear like a gazelle who is fleeing a wolf, and sped toward the willow tree where the youth awaited her. When she found herself by his side, she threw her arms about him and said tearfully, "My beloved, listen to me; I am sorry for having been hasty and thoughtless. I repented until my heart is crushed with sorrow; I love you and do not love any other; I shall continue to love you to the end of my life. They lied to me and told me that you loved another and Najeebee deceived me when she told me that you had fallen in love with her, and did so in order to induce me to accept her cousin as my bridegroom, as the family had long planned. I am married now but you are the only one I love and you are my bridegroom. Now that the veil has been removed from my eyes and truth is near, I came here to follow you to the end of life, and I will never go back to the man whom falsehood and narrow custom have selected for me as a husband. Let us hurry, my beloved, and leave this place under the protection of night. Let us go to the seacoast and embark upon a ship that will take us to a distant land where we will live together unmolested. Let us start now so when dawn comes we will be safe from the grip of the enemy; I have enough jewelry to take care of us for the rest of our lives . . . Why do you not talk, Saleem? Why do you not look at me? Why do you not kiss me? Are you listening to the wailing of my soul and the crying of my heart? Speak, and let us make haste to leave this place! The minutes we are losing are more precious than diamonds, and dearer than the crowns of the kings."

Her voice was more soothing than Life's whispering, and more anguished than the moaning call of Death, and softer than the rustling of wings, and deeper than the message of the waves . . . it was a voice that vibrated with hope and despair, with pleasure and pain, with happiness and misery, with need for life and desire for death. The youth was listening, but within him Love and Honor fought each other . . . Honor that confronts the spirit, and Love that God places in the human heart . . . After a long silence, the youth raised his head and turned his eyes away from the bride who was quivering with anxiety and he quietly protested, "Return to your destiny, for it is now too late. Sobriety has effaced what intoxication had painted. Go back before the guests see you here and say that you betrayed your husband on the wedding night just as you betrayed me during my absence." When she heard these words, she trembled like a withering flower before a tempest and she said painfully, "I shall never go back to that house which I have left forever. I feel now like a prisoner who leaves his exile . . . do not cast me from you, saying that I betrayed you. The hands that joined your heart and mine are stronger than the Emir's and the priest's hands which committed my body to my revolting bridegroom. There is no power that can take you from me . . . not even Death can separate our souls, for as Heaven has willed it, only Heaven can alter it."

Feigning disinterest and trying to free himself from the grip of her arms around him, Saleem retorted, "Depart from me! I love another with an intensity that causes me to forget you exist in this world. Najeebee was right when she told you that I loved her. Go back to your husband and be a faithful wife to him as the law commands."

The bride desperately protested, "No, no! I do not believe you, Saleem! I know that you love me, and I can read it in your eyes; I sense your love when I am close to you; I shall never leave you for my husband's home as long as my heart beats; I came here to follow you to the end of the world. Lead the way, Saleem, or shed my blood and take my life now." With a voice no stronger than before, Saleem returned, "Leave me, or I will shout and gather the people in this garden and disgrace you before God and man and let my beloved Najeebee laugh at you and be proud of her triumph."

As Saleem was endeavoring to unclasp her arms, she turned from a hopeful, kind, and pleading woman into a furious lioness who had lost her cubs, and she cried out saying, "No one shall ever triumph over me and take my love from me!" Having uttered these words, she drew a dagger from beneath her wedding gown, and swift as lightning, she sheathed it in the youth's heart. He fell upon the ground like a tender branch broken by the storms and she bent over him, holding the blood-stained dagger in her hand. He opened his eyes and his lips vibrated when he faltered, "Come now, my beloved; come, Lyla, and do not leave me. Life is weaker than Death, and Death is weaker than Love. Listen to the cruel laughter of the feasters inside the house, and hear the tinkling and breaking of the drinking cups, my beloved. Lyla, you have rescued me from Life's suffering. Let me kiss the hand that broke the chains and let me free. Kiss me and forgive me, for I have not been truthful.

"Place your blood-cleansed hands upon my withering heart, and when my soul ascends into the spacious sky, place the dagger in my right hand and say that I took my own life." He choked for breath and whispered, "I love you, Lyla, and never loved another. Self-sacrifice is nobler than fleeing with you. Kiss me, oh beloved sweetheart of my soul. Kiss me, oh Lyla . . ." And he placed his hand upon his wounded heart and breathed his last. The bride looked toward the house and cried in piercing agony, "Emerge from your stupor, for here is the wedding! The bride and the bridegroom are awaiting you! Come and see our soft bed! Wake up, you madmen and drunkards; hurry to this place so we can reveal to you the truth of Love, Death and Life!" Her hysterical voice rang through every corner of the house, echoing into the guests' ears. As if in a trance, they were drawn to the door and they walked out, looking in every direction. As they approached the scene of tragic beauty, and saw the bride weeping over Saleem, they retreated in fright and none dared come close by. It seemed that the stream of blood from the youth's heart, and the dagger in the bride's hand, had fascinated them and frozen the blood in their bodies. The bride looked at him and moaned bitterly, "Come, you cowards! Fear not the specter of Death whose greatness will refuse to approach your littleness, and dread not this dagger, for it is a divine instrument which declines to touch your filthy bodies and empty hearts. Look at this handsome youth . . . he is my beloved, and I killed him because I loved him . . . he is my bridegroom and I am his bride. We sought a bed worthy of our love in this world which you have made so small with your ignorance and traditions. But we chose this bed. Where is that wicked woman who slandered my beloved and said that he loved her? Where is the one who believed she triumphed over me? Where is Najeebee, that hell-viper who deceived me? Where is the woman who gathered you here to celebrate my beloved's departure and not the wedding of the man she had chosen for me? My words are vague to you, for the abyss cannot understand the song of the stars. You shall tell your children that I killed my beloved on the wedding night. My name shall be upon your dirty lips uttered with blasphemy, but your grandchildren shall bless me, for Tomorrow shall be for the freedom of truth and the spirit. And you, my ignorant husband, who bought my body but not my love, and who owns me but will never possess me, you are the symbol of this miserable nation, seeking light in darkness, and awaiting the coming of water from the rock; you symbolize a country ruled by blindness and stupidity; you represent a false humanity which cuts throats and arms in order to reach for a necklace or bracelet. I forgive you now, for the happy, departing soul forgives the sins of all the people."

Then the bride lifted her dagger toward the sky, and like a thirsty person who brings the edge of a drinking glass to his lips, she brought it down and planted it in her bosom. She fell by the side of her beloved like a lily whose flower was cut off by a sharp scythe. The women gazed upon the horrible scene and cried frightfully; some of them fell into a swoon, and the uproar of the men filled the sky. As they shamefully and reverently approached the victims, the dying bride looked at them, and with blood streaming from her stricken body, she said, "Stay away from us and separate not our bodies, for if you commit such a sin, the spirit that hovers over your heads will grasp you and take your lives. Let this hungry earth swallow our bodies and hide us in its bosom. Let it protect us as it protects the seeds from the snow until Spring comes, and restores pure life and awakening."

She came close to her beloved, placed her lips upon his cold lips, and uttered her last words, "Look, my forever . . . look at our friends. How the jealous are gathering about our bed! Hear the grating of their teeth and the crushing of their fingers! You have waited for me a long time, Saleem, and here I am, for I have broken the chains and shackles. Let us go toward the sun, for we have been waiting too long in this confining, dark world. All objects are disappearing from my sight and I can see naught but you, my beloved. These are my lips, my greatest earthly possession . . . accept my last human breath. Come, Saleem, let us leave now. Love has lifted his wings and ascended into the great light." She dropped her head upon his bosom and her unseeing eyes were still open and gazing upon him.

Silence prevailed, as if the dignity of death had stolen the people's strength and prevented them from moving. Whereupon the priest who had performed the wedding ceremony came forth and pointed with his forefinger at the death-bound couple shouting, "Cursed are the hands that touch these blood-spattered carcasses that are soaked with sin. And cursed are the eyes that shed tears of sorrow upon these two evil souls. Let the corpse of the son of Sodom and that of the daughter of Gomorrah remain lying in this diseased spot until the beasts devour their flesh and the wind scatters their bones. Go back to your homes and flee from the pollution of these sin-

93

ners! Disperse now, before the flames of hell sting you, and he who remains here shall be cursed and excommunicated from the Church and shall never again enter the temple and join the Christians in offering prayers to God!"

Susan, who acted as the last messenger between the bride and her beloved, walked forth bravely and stood before the priest. She looked at him with tearful eyes and said, "I shall remain here, you merciless heretic, and I shall guard them until dawn comes. I shall dig a grave for them under these hanging branches and bury them in the garden of their last earthly kiss. Leave this place immediately, for the swine detest the aromatic scent of incense, and the thieves fear the lord of the house and dread the coming of the brilliant sunrise. Hurry to your obscured beds, for the hymns of the angels will not enter your ears, blocked with the hardened cement of cruel and stupid rules."

The throng departed slowly with the stern-faced priest, and Susan remained watching over Lyla and Saleem as a loving mother guards her children in the silence of the night. When the multitude vacated the place, she dropped down and wept with the crying angels.